Website: www.allthingscynthiayoung.com

Email: info@glowingingrace.me

YouTube: **@GraceAcademyTV**

Follow us on social media **@GraceAcademyBR**

This Book Belongs To

Name: ____

Phone: _________________________   **Date:** _________________________

Email: ____

Greetings and Welcome to Guidance with Grace!

The Guidance with Grace Career Success Guide was created with you in mind and from a place of love and concern for my community. Working with individuals to help them achieve personal and professional success is what I love doing. I'm passionate about helping people to achieve success in life, work, and in school. I love to inspire people to take action on their goals. I do this through my writing, my books, coaching, mentoring, teaching, and community outreach.

As a Life Coach, I've been for others who I wish I had when I was navigating my way through college and different jobs that didn't give me a sense of purpose and fulfilment. After leaving high school in my junior year without a high school diploma, it wasn't until 10 years later before I returned to school to finish. I know what it feels like to be confused and not know how to navigate through my career journey with confidence and clarity.

What I share in this Career Success Guide is not always evident to the average person who's navigating their personal career path. This Career Success Guide is designed to help you identify and achieve your career goals with Grace & Ease.

The Career Success Guide contains several important aspects of career readiness including self-assessments and activities to help guide you toward finding meaningful work aligned with who you are and your purpose. With a consistent focus on positive identity, the activities in the guide reinforce both social-emotional and employability skills to support personal and professional achievement for individuals who are navigating their personal career path.

The Career Guide offers a variety of clarity questions to help individuals discover new information and practice new skills in relationship to their job and career development.

Authentically Yours,

Cynthia Young, MPA

Author | Life Coach | Teacher

"When you learn, teach,
when you get, give."
Maya Angelou

Contents

SMARTER Career Goal

SMARTER GOALS

Setting Goals

A goal is an aim or target that you work toward with effort and determination; an anticipated end result. Setting specific, measurable goals can provide a path to improve your career and achieve certain accomplishments. You can use goal setting when given a certain task or project, or to personally advance in some way. You can set goals towards promotions, creativity, education, and many other various ways to improve your life and career.

Let's look at why setting goals can help improve your career, what types of goals you can set and how to set goals.

Why Setting Goals Is Important

Setting goals is important because it gives you a framework to achieve milestones. Wanting to do or complete certain things in life is a great start. Goal setting provides a path for you to actually do them. There are two types of goals you should consider setting: short term and long term.

What Are The Short-Term Goals?

Short-term goals are more immediate goals you set for yourself to achieve your larger, long-term goals. You can think of short-term goals as milestones or stepping stones. Short-term goals usually exist in a short timeframe, anywhere from days or months to one or two years. Examples of short-term goals might include completing small tasks or projects, gaining experience, or taking classes. You will use what you accomplished in the short term to complete your long-term goals.

What Are Long-Term Goals?

Long-term goals are usually large goals you want to achieve over several years. You will use several milestones to achieve long-term goals, setting short-term goals to achieve along the way. Long-term goals might include getting a job in a certain career, being promoted to a certain level, or completing a lengthy, complicated project.

Setting Personal Goals

Setting goals for your personal life will help you reach personal achievements. You might set personal goals to advance several categories in your life for things like hobbies, health, or education. Setting personal goals can help you achieve success in your career as well.

I am committed to achieving success in every area of my life...

Affirm

What Are SMARTER Goals?

Let's quickly just go through the ones we already know…

S - Specific

Your goals need to be specific. They need to provide you with clarity and a concise aim as to where you are going with your objective. Ask yourself some of these questions to flesh out what your goal really is:

- ❖ What do I want to achieve?
- ❖ Is it likely I will face any challenges and what may these challenges be?
- ❖ How will I achieve this?

M - Measurable

Your goals need to be measurable. Giving yourself a metric to work alongside makes achieving your goals easier. You can create a timeline and benchmark your progress along it to see if you are meeting your goals in time or not. Ask yourself:

- ❖ Do I have a timeline?
- ❖ When do I want to achieve this goal?
- ❖ How will I know when I have accomplished this goal?

A - Achievable

Your goals need to be achievable. Are your goals realistic? Is it feasible for you to achieve them in the given timeframe? We like to think that we can achieve big targets, but sometimes this just isn't the case. Make your goals big enough to push yourself when trying to achieve them. But don't make them unachievable.

- ❖ Is this goal realistic?

R - Relevant

Your goals should be relevant. Every goal should have a reason behind it. Why is this goal significant to your life?

❖ Is the task worthwhile?

T - Timely

Make sure you set deadlines to your goals. It is harder to achieve timely goals without one. You may want to extend this to have a timeline of deadlines. Breaking down your goal into smaller ones so you can track your progress along the way.

❖ When is my task deadline?

❖ Should I create a timeline? If so, what are my smaller goals?

❖ What can I achieve in 6 months?

So, what about the new letters? Let's take a look…

E – Evaluate!

As opposed to winging it and hoping that by the end of the process you have achieved your goals, continuously evaluate your goals all the way along the process. This can differ by person. Some people may want to evaluate the progress of their goal daily, some weekly and some bi-monthly. Whatever you prefer, make sure you are continuously evaluating your goals to help make sure you achieve them. This goal links very well with timely, in that you have a timeline-based approach to goal setting.

It also means evaluating your performance at the end of the process so that you can learn from your mistakes and optimize your next goal setting process. Evaluating your goals will help you stay focused all the way along the process.

R – Readjust!

Ever been faced with a continuous problem in the workplace, are you hitting the wall? Well this letter is here to help you. If you are facing a continuous problem with your goals, it's time to take a step back and re-adjust. Re-adjusting doesn't mean throw away the goals and get new ones, it's a means to an end, a way of getting around your problems.

Clarity Questions

---

1. How do you define success?

2. What is something you want to accomplish in the next year?

3. Identify 10 accomplishments (successes) from your life.

4. What characteristics help people achieve success? What helped you in the examples of accomplishments that you just identified? (Confidence, determination, motivation, practice, responsibility, positive attitude, believing you can do it, having a clear goal, etc.)

MY SMARTER GOALS

Today's Date: _______________________   Target Date: _______________________

Date Achieved: _______________________   Start Date: _______________________

Goal: ____

____

Verify that your goal is SMARTER

Specific: What exactly will you accomplish?

____

____

Measurable: How will you know when you have reached this goal?

____

____

Achievable: Is achieving this goal realistic with effort and commitment? Have you got the resources to achieve this goal? If not, how will you get them?

____

____

Relevant: Why is this goal significant to your life?

____

____

Timely: When will you achieve this goal?

____

____

Evaluate: Check the progress of your goal; daily, weekly, or monthly?

____

____

Readjust: Approach your goal from a different angle if needed?

____

____

This goal is important because:

____

____

The benefits of achieving this goal will be:

____

____

____

Specific Action Steps: What steps need to be taken to get you to your goal?

What?	Expected Completion	Date Completed
__________________	______________	______________
__________________	______________	______________
__________________	______________	______________

Real-World Application

Share at least one short term goal with three people in your life and ask them to support you in reaching your goal — and check in to make sure you are sticking to your plan.

Available Resources

Cold Resources

- ❖ What equipment might be necessary to achieve your goal?
- ❖ What do you have already?
- ❖ What could you borrow?
- ❖ What do you need to buy?
- ❖ What facility space do you need to achieve your goal?
- ❖ What do you need to do to create a space or find a space?

Warm Resources

- ❖ What people in your life can in anyway help you achieve your goal?
- ❖ How could they help you?
- ❖ What skill or trade would be helpful for someone to have that was willing to help you?
- ❖ Who do you know that could support you in achieving your goal? (encouragement, money, connections)
- ❖ Which people with what kind of experience would be helpful to you in achieving your goal?

Intellectual Resources

- ❖ What do you need to research before making a plan on how you are going to achieve your goal?
- ❖ What information would be helpful to have before you make a plan on how to achieve your goal?

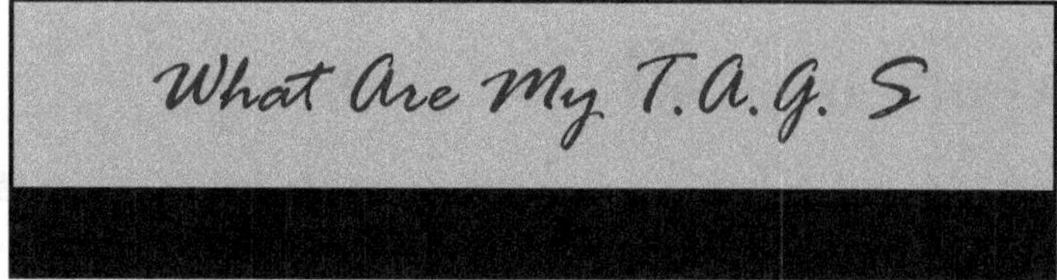

Your skillset consists of your own **talents, abilities, gifts, and skills**. Abilities and strengths can be inborn characteristics and talents or skills you have learned over the course of your life. You may have enhanced your skills through study, work experience, hobbies or in relationships. Think through your own skillset using the following questions:

My talents are:

____

____

I possess the following abilities:

____

____

What are some of your gifts and skills: (spiritual & non spiritual)

____

____

How do I typically do things? For instance, when you want to sort something out, do you look to the Internet or to books, do you phone a friend, or do you think about it on your own? Do you usually do things alone or together with others?

What have you learned through work?

What skills and knowledge have you acquired through studying?

What skills have you acquired through your hobbies and whatever else you do in your spare time?

Choose the three most important skills or strengths that you have identified through this exercise.

____

____

____

Ask yourself: What abilities and skills do I want to develop in myself?

____

____

____

I have something special to offer the world...

Affirm

Exploring My Values

What makes people show up for work every day? One obvious answer is — a paycheck. But money isn't all that people want from work. In fact, research shows that most people think some things are more important than money. People who like their work — and there really are millions of them — usually, rate pay as the # 8 value in a list of 10. Some things people might value more than money are recognition for doing a good job, working as part of a team, building something people need, or helping people improve their lives.

What would make you show up for work every day? Once you have a regular paycheck, you'll want satisfying work to keep you coming back. The aim of this lesson is to discover your work values — the things you want to get from work to feel it's worth the effort. When your work fits with your values, work isn't just a way to pay the bills; it's fulfilling and exciting.

Once you identify which values are most important, think about the kinds of work that would provide them. That's an important step in making career decisions that will be right for you.

As children, most people have dreams about what they want to be when they grow up. What jobs sounded good to you when you were a child? As you get older, you may no longer want that dream, or may feel that it is unrealistic, but you may still want some of the values those dreams represent. Complete the following activities.

1. When I was younger, I wanted to be a ____

2. In the list below, "My Values," circle the values, or reasons, why you wanted that job/career.

3. Look at the list again. Write five (5) values that are most important to you today. Have your values changed?

______________________   ______________________   ______________________

______________________   ______________________

My Values

Achievement	Power	High Income
Respect	Advancement	Creativity
Honesty	Security	Ambition
Influence	Service	Helpful
Knowledge	Status	Entrepreneur
Independence	Leadership	Team Work
Beauty	Excitement	Loyalty
Time Freedom	Friendship	Recognition
Trust	Challenge	Fame

Values are your principles or standards that guide your life and work. They signify what is important to you and are a measure by which you gauge success in your life.

Because your values are an important part of who you are, you will be more satisfied in your career when it aligns with your values. When you work and live out of alignment with your values, you end up being dissatisfied, frustrated, and discouraged.

Because you'll change and grow as a person, your values can and should change over time. This means your career choices can and should change over time too. Take time to reflect on the things that truly matter to you, to figure out your values.

6 Core Work Value Areas

Achievement

- ❖ Something done successfully, typically by effort, courage, or skill

Independence

- ❖ Freedom from the control, influence, support, aid, or the like, of others.

Recognition

- ❖ To acknowledge someone or something; praise, respect, or admiration; agreement something is true or important.

Relationships

- ❖ The state of being connected.

Support

- ❖ 1. An act or instance of helping. 2. To hold up or serve as a foundation for.

Working Conditions

- ❖ Refers to the working environment and conditions of your work. This covers matters such as: work activities; training, skills, health, safety, and well-being.

Clarity Questions

---

1. What are the emotional and opportunity consequences if you wait to take action for another year? Five years?

2. How is choosing not to take action causing you extra pain and violating your values? (Pain can be physical, emotional, financial, or even wasted resources like time or energy, etc.)

3. Who else is suffering because you're allowing yourself to stay stuck in your current work situation? Your partner? Your friends? Your children? Your community?

4. If you stay in this job, what does that say about your priorities and values? What kind of example is that setting for your current or future children, nieces, and nephews, etc.?

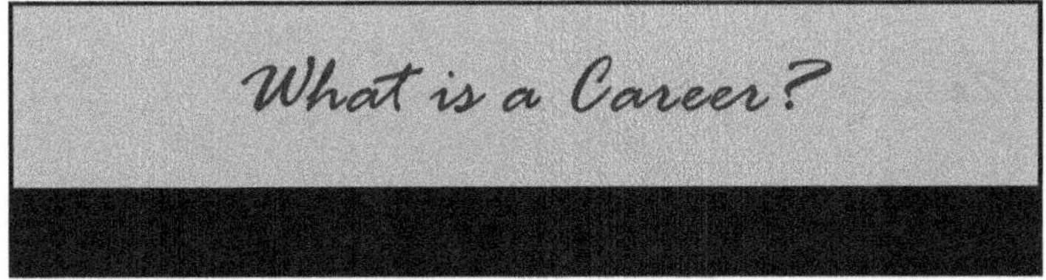

What Is A Career?

A **career** is the job or profession that someone does for a long period of their life. **A career** could define what you do for a living and range from those that require extensive training and education to those you can perform with only a high school diploma and a willingness to learn. **A career** could mean working as a doctor, lawyer, teacher, carpenter, veterinary assistant, electrician, cashier, teacher, or hairstylist.

Work Is A Blessing From God!

Work is God-ordained, and it allows us to use the skills, intelligence, and experience that He has gifted us. In Genesis, we see God working to create the earth. We also see God put Adam in charge of the Garden of Eden to take care of it.

I'm giving God something to Bless...

affirm

We Were Created to Work

When people aren't working, studies show an increase in the following areas:

Economical	Societal	Psychological
Poverty	Domestic Violence	Depression
Debt	Crime/Prison	Suicide
Homelessness	Recidivism	Anger

How we feel about our work has the possibility to infect every other part of our lives. Can you imagine what our world would look like if people enjoyed or even loved—their work? We would have more energy.

Studies show that doing work you're good at and that you enjoy gives you energy instead of sucking it away. More energy means more productivity within our jobs, more capacity to give to family and friends outside of work.

We'd feel motivated to exercise or play with our kiddos or write our first novel after work because we'd still have gas left in the tank. We'd perform better because we'd care more.

Research shows that performance at work improves by anywhere from 12-36% when you like your work and feel your contributions make a difference.

Better performance usually means more promotions, raises, eligibility for bonuses, additional challenging responsibilities, and higher job security.

Clarity Questions

Assessing Your Next Career Move

1. In your efforts to establish a career, list below what you have done that is Positive:

2. What more might you do at this time to further your career?

3. What is currently holding you back from doing it?

4. What realistically might you commit to do now?

Career Aspiration

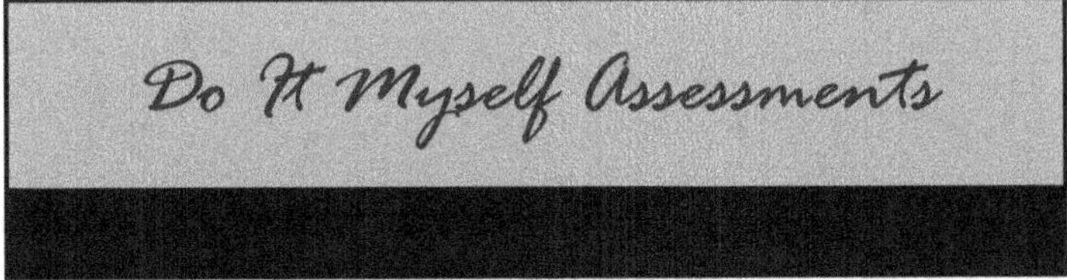

Self-Assessments 

Career Fitter Career Assessment (Free and Premium Version)

Discover your work personality strengths and best careers.

https://www.careerfitter.com/

16 Personalities Personality Assessment (Free and Premium Version)

This straightforward, illuminating assessment helps you define your ideal values in a career. It's a great way to measure your current situation and get some valuable perspective on where you are – and where you might want to go. Simple, easy-to-follow directions lead to a summary designed to aid your own evaluation of what matters to you. Most people can't get everything they want in a job, so it is a wise idea to prioritize the things that are most important to you.

https://www.16personalities.com/profile

O*NET Interest Profiler (Free Version)

The O*NET Interest Profiler can help you find out what your interests are and how they relate to the world of work. You can find out what you like to do. The O*NET Interest Profiler helps you decide what kinds of careers you might want to explore.

https://www.mynextmove.org/

More than half of U.S. workers are unhappy in their jobs. Studies show 3 out of 10 employees say that they are satisfied in their work.

Searching for a job can be stressful on its own. Not to mention the anxiety of convincing an employer that YOU are the right person for the position, especially during a time when opportunities are scarce or competitive. If you have little work experience, or if the bulk of your work experience has been in one specific area, you may feel unqualified for a different job or a career change. Good news: that isn't always true. The key is identifying the skills you already have and learning how to make them work for your résumé

General skills that you've gained from a previous role (whether you got paid for it or not), and that you can use in a variety of jobs, are called transferable skills. Being able to show potential employers that you can transfer the valuable skills you already have could make you an attractive candidate for more jobs than you may have thought.

In a survey of 500 US employers, the most desirable traits in job candidates are things like an ability to complete tasks, common sense, dependability, enthusiasm, motivation to achieve, and adaptability, just to name a few. Notice that these are all general attributes, and not job-specific duties or experience related qualities.

While some jobs do require very specific education or training, regardless of what type of job you're looking for, being able to isolate your transferable skills will only make your résumé stronger.

Make A List Of Your Skills

Someone who has worked on the same assembly line for years may feel like that's the only thing they can do. But when you take a deeper look, you see that working on that assembly line required skills like attention to detail, ability to maintain focus on a task for long periods of time, or quality control. Similarly, someone who has been a student for most of their life may not have any work experience, but their skills probably include things like meeting deadlines, creating presentations, and organizational skills. Try to zero in on all of the little things that helped you in your last role. Chances are those little things will add up to the kinds of skills that employers are looking for.

Look For "Hooks" In The Job Description

Just like the catchy line in a song that grabs your attention, job descriptions have hooks too. Look for key words or phrases and match them to your skills. For example, a job that is in a "fast paced environment" probably needs someone who works well under pressure, has excellent time management, or is able to stick to deadlines. Someone who has experience working in a restaurant or other areas of the service industry, for instance, likely has those skills already.

Be Able To Give Examples

Being able to back up the skills you list on your résumé is very important; don't be surprised if potential employers ask for concrete examples. It can be stressful being put on the spot, but don't panic! Fortunately, you've already done the hard work. Think back to the list you made of your skills. Which skill is it? Why did you put it on the list? When did you use it? How did it help you? Take time to answer these questions before an interview so you can be prepared if it comes up.

One last thing to remember: when it comes to résumé s and interviews; honesty is the best policy. When listing your skills, stick to the ones you know you can provide solid examples for.

Hard Skills vs. Soft Skills

When it comes to work skills, they can be broken down into two types: *hard skills and soft skills.* They're pretty different from one another, but both are necessary to be successful on the job.

- ❖ **Hard skills** are concrete skills that are specific to your job and are required for you to actually do your work. For example, if you're a chef, cooking would be a hard skill. Or if you're a computer programmer, coding would be an example.
- ❖ **Soft skills,** on the other hand, are interpersonal or people skills that can be used in every job. These include communication, teamwork, and adaptability.
- ❖ **Hard skills** are generally learned through school, training, or previous work experience. They're objective, meaning that once you've learned the information or task, you then possess that skill. Because of this, they're fairly easy to measure. Employers can get a good idea of your hard skills by looking at your certifications, education, and previous experience.
- ❖ **Soft skills** are a bit more difficult to develop than hard skills. You'll need to practice them over time in the real world with others. They come naturally to some people, while others may not have such an easy time with them.
- ❖ **Soft skills** are also harder to evaluate. They can't really be communicated well through your cover letter or résumé. Instead, employers usually have to wait until an interview or your first few weeks on the job to get a good idea of your soft skills.

Despite their differences, you'll need both hard and soft skills if you want to become more hirable or be successful in your current job.

Transferable Skills Include

Communication: Written, Verbal and Listening	Honesty and integrity	Self-motivation or initiative	Problem-solving abilities or an analytical mind
The ability to work on a team	Dependability	A capacity for leadership	Strong work ethic
Interpersonal skills and friendliness	The ability to handle stressful situations	Flexibility and adaptability	Organizational or time-management abilities
Critical Thinking	Basic computer knowledge	Proficiency in another language	Customer service

The more transferable skills you have, the more diversity you can offer to a potential employer.

Managing Your Money

Managing money can be hard to do. One look at the average credit debt for American families is enough to convince anyone of the difficulty of money management. Wouldn't it be nice if there were a magic formula or simple trick that allowed you never to have to worry about money or managing your finances again? While that may not be realistic, there are some simple things you can do right now to improve your money situation.

Detail Your Financial Goals

Take some time to write specific, long-term financial goals. Your goal to retire early is dependent on how well you save your money now. Other goals, including homeownership, starting a family, moving, or changing careers, will all be affected by how you manage your finances.

Once you have written down your financial goals; prioritize them. This organizational process ensures that you are paying the most attention to the ones that are of the highest importance to you.

Flesh out Your Plan

A financial plan is essential in helping you reach your financial goals. The plan should have multiple steps or milestones. A sample plan might include creating a monthly budget and spending plan, then getting out of debt.

When creating a financial plan, remember these things:

❖ Your budget is key to success. It is the tool that will give you the most control of your financial future. Your budget is the key to achieving the rest of your plan.

❖ You should keep contributing to long-term goals, like saving for retirement, no matter what your financial plan stage is.

Make and Stick to a Budget

Your budget is one of the biggest tools that will help you succeed financially. It allows you to create a spending plan so you can allocate your money in a way that will help you to reach your goals.

You can make your budget as high-level or detailed as you want, as long as it helps you reach your ultimate goal of spending less than you earn, paying off any debts, padding your emergency fund, and saving for the future.

A budget will also help you decide how to spend your money over the coming months and years. Without the plan, you might spend cash on things that seem important now, but don't offer much in terms of enhancing your future.

Financial Barriers

Personal and financial barriers are among the most difficult to overcome because they often prevent individuals from making choices or taking positive action. For example, it may be difficult for an individual to return to school if he or she cannot find childcare; or it may be difficult to search for jobs if that person has no reliable transportation. Therefore, it is often most important for people to overcome these personal and financial barriers before they can move on to identifying and eliminating other barriers.

Research has confirmed that people have to overcome their most basic barriers in order to be successful in life and in their career. Abraham Maslow was one of the first researchers to identify a hierarchy of needs that also can act as a hierarchy of barriers. At the lowest, most deficient level are many survival needs that correspond to the personal and financial barriers that this section of the workbook addresses. In order to reach higher levels of success, happiness, and self-actualization, those basic survival needs must first be met.

Financial Barriers and the Job Search

Financial barriers are at the heart of any job search. It is difficult for job seekers to think about employment when their family is hungry, when their pants have holes in them, or when they are living in their car.

If you are unemployed or struggling to stay employed, then you may not be concerned about your long-term financial future. But that doesn't mean that you shouldn't be. Financial goals should be at the heart of your career research. It should factor into all of your career planning and job acceptance decisions. Though it may not seem like a pressing need, having a long-term financial plan can positively impact your job search success.

Long-term financial success does not happen automatically. You need to make it happen. It is important for you to have a dream and work toward that dream.

I am living my life in a state of complete abundance…

Affirm

Clarity Questions

---

1. How can finances help or hinder your search for a job?

2. What are the best ways to manage money?

3 Why are budgets so difficult to stick to, and what can be done to make it easier to stick to a budget?

4. What role does your family play in your job search? What contributions do they make, both positive and negative?

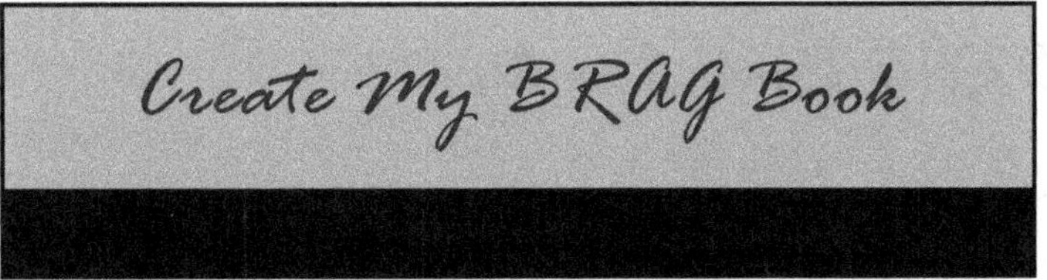

Be Recognized for Advancement and Growth

A BRAG *(Be Recognized for Advancement and Growth)* Book is an excellent way to visually showcase your accomplishments. While portfolios are expected in certain "creative" professions, jobseekers in many more "traditional" fields could benefit from preparing a BRAG Book to use in an interview. Not only is it an excellent way to prepare for a job interview, but it is also an excellent confidence booster! There's just something about seeing all of your accomplishments in print that boosts your confidence and self-esteem.

Creating a BRAG Book will give your résumé much more credibility because you are able to show actual proof of your key contributions and accomplishments you have showcased in your document. A BRAG Book is an excellent tool to take to interviews for a number of reasons.

First off, by being able to show proof of what you say you did, you will boost your chances of moving through the process.

For instance, if the employer asks about your experience in a particular area and you have some related accomplishments, you could whip out your BRAG Book and hand them that piece of information to review on the spot. This will remove any doubt in the mind of the interviewer that they may have had about your experience.

It's also a good tool to start a conversation about your career success stories in the event that the conversation kind of lags or the hiring authority is talking too much and not giving you an opportunity to really shine.

What Is A BRAG Book Exactly?

A BRAG Book isn't reserved just for creative types – virtually anyone in any type of profession can create one. All it needs to be is a well-organized and professionally presented file that gives concrete proof of your achievements which could also include samples of some of your best work. It's recommended that you have both a physical file such as a binder as well as a digital file in the event that it needs to be emailed to a hiring authority.

The kinds of things you include in your BRAG Book will depend on what you have to show, but it could be photos, reports, marketing collateral (brochures), correspondence, and other things.

It's important that your BRAG Book be well organized, neat, and professional looking. This isn't something you want to whip together at the last second. In fact, doing this properly will take some time, so don't rush it.

For the physical portfolio, I recommend using a good quality binder and organize the contents by including a tables of contents, using dividers to break up content into categories, and also protect each document in plastic sleeves.

For a digital presentation, I recommend that you create a slide deck that has a crisp, clean, and professional look.

What To Include In Your BRAG Book

The general rule of thumb is to include anything that you can think of that makes you look good and helps to communicate your unique value proposition.

- ❖ Performance reviews from current/former employers
- ❖ Awards/ Rewards Letters (official recognition of doing a good job)
- ❖ Letters of recommendation
- ❖ Congratulatory notes (anything that compliments you on doing a great job from employers, co-workers, customers, clients)

- ❖ Feedback/Testimonials/Endorsements
- ❖ Certificates of completion of career-relevant educational courses, workshops, seminars
- ❖ College/University transcripts (only if you're a new grad and your marks are good)
- ❖ Community or Organizational Involvement
- ❖ List of specific accomplishments that are not on your résumé

Review your materials to prioritize what to include. Create a logical order and structure for your BRAG Book. This can be reverse chronological or by section. Start with your most recent accomplishment and work backwards. Ensure that the physical copies that you make are good quality and legible. Presentation is everything!

Consider creating sections to make it easy to navigate. If dividing the BRAG Book into sections, use professional divider tabs. You can purchase these in an office supply store. Generally, a 5-tab or 8-tab configuration is sufficient.

Do not include original documents in your BRAG Book (except for your résumé). This way, if you are asked for your transcript, for example, you're giving the interviewer a copy (one of several you've made), not your only copy (your original).

Proofread and edit carefully. Review all the materials in your BRAG Book for typos, spelling, grammar, and formatting issues.

When possible, tailor your BRAG Book specifically for a desired job. If you use a 3-ring binder with page protector sheets, you can simply insert the pages you want to include for a particular job interview. For example, if the position requires public speaking skills, include a photo of you delivering a presentation to a large crowd. If the position does not require presentation skills, then you could leave that page out.

For maximum results, personalize the BRAG Book — especially if it's a leave-behind piece. Building your BRAG Book from scratch will take some time, but you can start small and improve it over time.

Benefits Of The BRAG Book

Even though you might not need a BRAG Book, it's a good idea to take one with you in the event an opportunity arises for you to reference an example of something you did particularly well.

Going through the process of creating your BRAG Book will boost your self-confidence when you see how many times you made a positive impact in your career. This will make you feel more positive every time you go into an interview and reduce your performance anxiety, knowing that you have evidence literally at your fingertips that you can produce to show your worth.

This is particularly important if the job search is taking longer than anticipated and eroding your confidence. Being able to reflect on your career successes will give you the morale boost that you need to soldier on through what could be a challenging process.

But more importantly, taking an impressive-looking work BRAG Book with you into the interview will show that you are well-prepared and have gone the extra mile which will make you stand out from the other candidates.

At the end of the day, it's the little things that can make a world of difference.

Career Connection

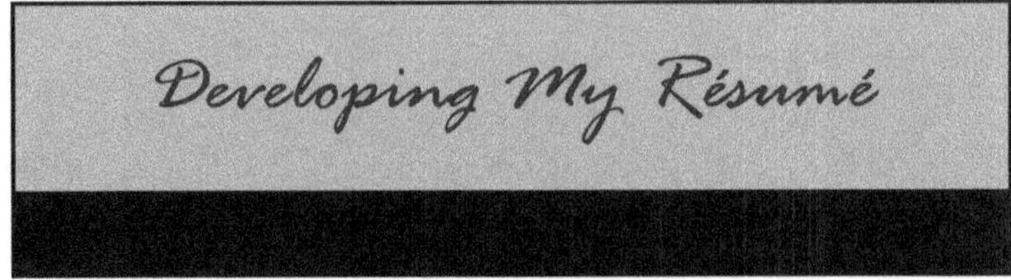

Why You Need A Résumé

Finding employment can be challenging for anyone, but the job market can be especially tough for recent college graduates, people re-entering the workforce after time away, or someone who has been in a position for a long time. Competition is stiff; the market is filled with other strong job candidates, too. So how can you increase your chances for getting a great job in the field you love? For almost everyone, it starts with a résumé.

A résumé is a document that you put together to sell your skills and experience to a hiring manager when you are trying to get a specific job. Hiring managers scan numerous résumés to find the few candidates who most closely match the needs of their organizations. They usually meet with these candidates for interviews to determine which candidate to hire.

A résumé is part of your professional brand. You'll know your résumé is in good shape if you are getting contacted for interviews. A recruiter typically screens a résumé within a matter of seconds; therefore, it's important to strategically position your content in an appealing format.

The same basic information should be included on each résumé, regardless of which résumé format is used. The information you should include is:

- ❖ Your **Contact Information**, so a hiring manager can easily get in touch with you if needed.

- ❖ A **Professional Summary**, sometimes called a **profile** that gives the hiring manager a glimpse of your skills and accomplishments.

- ❖ Your **Employment History**, which should provide specific details about the accomplishments and successes you've had in your previous jobs. It always includes the names and locations of the employer and should include a job title that is generally understandable. Dates are often included in this section, although you may want to omit them if you have gaps in your employment history.

- ❖ Your **Education** information, which should include the certifications or degrees you have earned, the institutions from which you earned them, and the dates they were awarded.

- ❖ Any **Additional Skills and Information** that highlight any technical or specialized skills you have that are applicable to the position.

Résumé Formats: Choosing The Right One

With hiring managers and other staffing professionals spending so little time on your résumé in their first pass, it is crucial to make sure your résumé makes the best initial impression. One way to do this is to choose the résumé format that best highlights your experience, education, and skills.

Let's explore the various ways key information is presented in chronological, functional, and combination résumés.

A Chronological Résumé

- ❖ Includes job titles, dates of employment, and a description of the job in terms of accomplishments and measurable tasks

❖ Is most often done in reverse order, with your most recent job listed first

❖ Works best for job seekers who have a steady employment history or previous employment that is related to the position being sought

The Functional Résumé

A less popular résumé format among recruiters and hiring staff is the functional résumé that highlights your skills without revealing the dates associated with your job history. The functional résumé minimizes specific job titles and eliminates dates of employment while emphasizing your abilities and skills by placing them in functional skill categories.

The functional résumé works well if you:

❖ Have worked many different jobs or possess very diverse skills
❖ Have skills that relate to the position, but not a lot of previous work experience in the field
❖ Have gaps in employment history, are a recent graduate, or are changing careers
❖ Are a mature worker and want to de-emphasize your age

Many hiring managers dislike the functional résumé because they can't use it to gauge your reliability, longevity, or how recently you used certain skills. For example, someone who created sales brochures 20 years ago may not be familiar with the software technologies used to produce a sales brochure today.

The Combination Résumé

The combination résumé is pretty rare. Like the chronological format, the combination résumé details your work experience, starting with your current or most recent position and ending with your oldest. Like a functional résumé, it also prominently displays your relevant and useful skills and accomplishments. This format works well for job seekers who:

❖ May have obtained the required skills from seemingly unrelated industries or jobs

❖ Are trying to change careers and want to emphasize transferable skills

❖ Have had a steady work history

Tips For Writing A Great Résumé

Consider using the following techniques as you approach writing your résumé.

❖ **Customize your résumé for each position you are applying for**. Use your summary or profile section to **highlight** your skills and expertise as they relate to the specific job. Better yet, carry this customization throughout the entire résumé. It may be convenient to create several versions of your résumé based on common positions you will be applying for so you can eliminate the amount of customization you will have to do for each job.

❖ **Include key words on your résumé**. Keep the job description close by when you are customizing your résumé so you are including key words and phrases that fit the job, field, or occupation. Recruiters often scan a résumé in under 15 seconds. They are looking for key words that show you have the skills and knowledge required for the position.

❖ **Be concise**. Because some recruiters look at as many as 500 résumés to fill one position, they want to see your accomplishments, skills, and experiences in as few words as possible. Bullet points and concise language can showcase your communication skills while highlighting your areas of expertise.

❖ **List your past work accomplishments (not just your responsibilities) using some form of measures**. Hiring managers want to compare your skills and abilities to the other candidates they are considering.

Tips For Designing A Great Résumé.

You now have some strategies for how to write and phrase your text, but the way you design and format your résumé for clarity and readability can be just as important.

Consider using the following techniques as you approach the design of your résumé.

- ❖ **Use white space and bullet points to help emphasize what you want the hiring manager to know about you**. If the hiring manager is scanning to see if you meet the requirements but can't easily spot the information, you may get overlooked.

- ❖ **Use bold and italics** to emphasize key words or skills. Be careful to not overuse this technique, though. If there are too many elements in bold or italics, the emphasis is lost.

- ❖ **Use a larger-point font** for headings and subheadings. This can help direct attention to certain areas of your résumé and also demonstrates a strong level of organization.

- ❖ **Use a conservative font**, like Times New Roman, Arial, or Tahoma. If the font is difficult to read, your résumé may not get past the first look.

- ❖ **Include adequate white space**. This can be done around your headings, blocks of text, and with margins. Hiring managers can use this area to take notes before, during, or after an interview.

Carefully Edit Your Text. Consider These Tips.

- ❖ **Use verb tense consistently**. For your present job, you can use the present tense, such as **design and oversee production of building additions**. For previous employment, use the past tense (**designed and oversaw**).

- ❖ **Vary your word choice**. Even though you are trying to include key words, don't overdo it. If the key phrase you are trying to include is **strategic**

planning, use a thesaurus to find alternative words, like **defined program goals and measures**.

❖ **Spell check, spell check, and spell check!** Almost every recruiter and hiring manager has a story about the résumé they threw out because of a misspelled word. Typos and misspelled words show that you are not detail oriented about your work. However, do not rely on your spell-checking software alone. Some grammar and spelling mistakes can be easily missed.

Common Résumé Mistakes To Avoid

There are several reasons hiring managers consistently put résumés in the **No** pile. You want to avoid these common mistakes.

❖ **Don't submit your résumé for a position for which you are not qualified**. This was cited as the No. 1 pet peeve among HR professionals on a recent LinkedIn discussion. Make sure you meet at least the basic requirements. Think creatively, though, because sometimes the work you have performed outside of the field may help you meet job requirements.

❖ **Don't lie**. Whether or not it's intentional, including false, inaccurate, or misleading information brings your ethics into question and can even be illegal. Keep in mind that hiring managers are much more likely to Google and/or conduct background checks on candidates to eliminate dishonest ones.

❖ **Don't disregard references**. While you do not need to post your reference information on your résumé, you should at least have them listed in a separate document that can be easily supplied if requested. Make sure your references are willing and ready to discuss your skills and abilities with a potential employer.

❖ **Don't use more than two fonts**. This can make a document difficult to read. The reader's eye needs familiar and easy-to-read fonts, like Times New Roman and Tahoma.

❖ **Don't use clip art on your résumé**. Clip art is not generally considered professional, and any style or formatting design should be minimal. However, if you are applying for a job in a creative industry, then showcasing your design abilities on your résumé may be more acceptable and appealing.

❖ **Don't include pictures**. Unless it is required for the position, your photo is not necessary.

❖ **Don't include personal or health-related information**. This includes your birth date, height and weight, health or marital status, religion, or affiliations in clubs that are not related to your career. While it may be appropriate in other cultures and for certain jobs, personal information should generally not be included if you are submitting a résumé for a job in the United States.

❖ **Don't include salary information** unless you are specifically asked to do so.

❖ **Don't misspell anything**. Misspelling words, especially words about the position, make you appear careless and unreliable. Use a spell checker and have at least two other people proofread your résumé for typos and errors.

My perfect career opportunity is on its way to me...

Affirm

Preparing Your Résumé For The Internet 

Linking To Online Profiles And Personal Websites

With the growth of social media, blogs, and personal webpages, it is now becoming more common to see these links on résumés. Webpage portfolios, LinkedIn profiles, and blogs have the capacity to showcase more about who you are and the type of work you have done.

Some professionals believe links can enhance a résumé by allowing a potential employer to go online and find out more about a candidate. However, there are some drawbacks to putting these links on your résumé, especially if your webpage or profile is not polished and professional.

Here Are A Few Things To Consider

- ❖ **Webpage portfolios** are great for showcasing your work, especially if you are in a technical or creative industry. They can be especially beneficial for college graduates and entry-level job hunters who may not have the work experience to prove their abilities.

- ❖ **Blogs** are another way to highlight your personality and expertise. They are a good alternative for those whose careers may not produce actual physical work samples to showcase. However, keep in mind that blogs are very opinion-oriented and can open you up to negative comments or feedback that potential employers can read.

- ❖ **Online professional profiles**, such as LinkedIn, offer the advantages of highlighting your expertise, posting related links, and offering recommendations from colleagues all conveniently located in one spot. However, you should once again consider that the social interactive nature of profiles makes it difficult to control all of the content on your page, which may make you vulnerable to content you would not like a potential employer to read.

❖ **Online social media sites** like Twitter and Facebook should only be linked if you use them for professional branding and networking rather than for personal social interaction. Also, if you do not have much of a following on these sites, it will not be advantageous to include them. Only a professional profile with a strong following will portray you as an expert in your field.

❖ **Maintain an updated, professional, and polished site** if you are going to use one of these links on your résumé. Make sure all content is grammatically correct. Create design and formatting that is professional and appealing. Remove all content that may be considered personal and/or inappropriate in nature.

❖ **Photos** are commonly expected on profile sites and are a great advantage for potential employers; however, they may make you vulnerable to discrimination based on your physical appearance.

A majority of job hunting is now conducted online, which means you need to understand the rules and strategies for emailing and posting your résumé on the Internet. Protecting your identity and making sure your résumé gets through online are two important concerns for job seekers. After all, you've spent a lot of time preparing your résumé, so you want to make sure it is effectively received by potential employers without having to sacrifice your privacy.

Format Your Résumé For Privacy And Online Posting

Save it as a PDF

- ❖ Learn the importance of saving your résumé as a pdf

- ❖ Follow along step by step for how to convert your résumé from a word document or google doc to a pdf

- ❖ Access free tools to help you convert your documents to pdf

Emailing Your Résumé

Because most correspondence with potential employers is now conducted by email, it is important for you to understand how to send your résumé online. With some jobs, you can simply attach your résumé to the email. However, some companies and hiring managers avoid attachments from untrusted sources due to the possibility of obtaining viruses from the attachment.

So how do you send your résumé via email?

The job posting will usually give instructions for submitting your résumé. If attachments are not allowed, you'll need to create a plain-text version of your résumé and copy and paste it into the body of your email.

Do It Yourself 🖥 Résumé Worksheet

Contact Information

____

Name

____

Address

____

City   State   Zip

____

Phone Number   Alternate Phone Number   E-mail

Employment Goal

What is your objective or job target?

____

What industry do you want to work in? (Construction, finance, maintenance and repair, hotel/hospitality, human services, healthcare, education, etc.)

Skills
List all your skills (if you speak another language that is also a skill) and your strengths. For computer skills include software that you know. (Example: Microsoft Word, Excel, Internet Applications, etc.)

____

Job Readiness Level

Education Information

____

Name of your school

Town/location of your school

Year you will be graduating

Awards

List all awards that you have ever received. If you were involved in sports also list any medals you may have won. (E.g.: perfect attendance, gold in 100 m hurdles)

Certificates

List any certifications you have ever received. (E.g.: CPR, First Aid, Workplace Readiness, etc.)

List any student activities or internships here:

Work History and Volunteer Experience

List your work history and/or volunteer history starting with your most recent job/volunteer work.

Start   End   Name of company

City and State

Your Title/Position

Describe what you did on the job (action words)

____

____

Start   End   Name of company

____
City and State

____
Your Title/Position

Describe what you did on the job (action words)

____

____

Start   End   Name of company

____
City and State

____
Your Title/Position

Describe what you did on the job (action words)

____

I have confidence in my decisions...

Affirm

You've found the job you want and have spruced up your résumé in hopes of getting it. Now all you have to do is submit it, right? Not so fast! Every résumé should have a great cover letter to go with it.

So What's A Cover Letter?

As the name implies, a cover letter is a document that introduces you and accompanies your résumé. It is what a hiring manager will see first.

In a competitive job market, hiring managers may get hundreds of résumés for only one position. Going through all of them can be time consuming. To alleviate the time strain, most hiring managers will quickly read over or scan cover letters to decide which résumés to read more closely.

Benefits of Providing A Cover Letter

- ❖ Demonstrate how well you express yourself and that you have researched the organization and position

- ❖ Tell prospective employers what position you're interested in, why you are interested in it, and how you came to know about it

- ❖ Highlight a few key skills that demonstrate your qualifications for the specific organization and position

- ❖ Thank the hiring manager in advance for her time and consideration

Both résumé and cover letters should be customized for each specific job opportunity. If you see a job posting that requests a résumé, send both a cover letter and résumé.

Include a cover letter every time you submit a résumé for a job, even if you are emailing it or uploading it to a job board!

Parts Of A Cover Letter

A cover letter is really a formal business letter that acts as an introduction to your résumé. Because it is a formal business document, it should be in block business letter format. In this format, text is left justified (aligned on the left-hand margin).

- ❖ **Date**: This is the date the letter is written.

- ❖ **Greeting:** The greeting is an important part of your cover letter. It establishes who you are sending the résumé and cover letter to. Try to find the name of the hiring manager to use here. If you can't find a name, use a generic term like Staff Selection Team or Hiring Manager.

- ❖ **Body**: The body is the main part of your cover letter. This is where you explain what job you are interested in and how you learned about it. It should also present you as the best possible candidate for the job and explain what actions you will take next.

- ❖ **Close**: Use a polite and professional phrase here, such as Sincerely, Respectfully, or Kind Regards.

- ❖ **Signature**: This area should contain your name, a written signature (if you're mailing the letter), and another way to contact you (such as a phone number or email address).

Clarity Questions

---

1. What are your "Why, How, and Now?

2. What's the driving force behind your work?

3. How does it feel when you share it?

4. What are the most important and relevant accomplishments from your past career experiences to share?

Cover Letter Tips

The following are some tips to make your cover letter the best it can be.

- ❖ Gather all necessary information first. This includes the job description, name of the hiring manager, and any other research you have gathered about the company.
- ❖ Follow directions. Some employers may want you to provide additional materials, such as writing samples, with your résumé. Others might not accept applications that are sent via email. Before you respond to any job posting, read the directions carefully so you can provide exactly what is required.
- ❖ Address your letter to a specific individual. If this is not possible, use a gender-neutral greeting, like *Dear Hiring Manager* or *Staff Selection Team.*
- ❖ Write a rough draft
- ❖ Consider using résumé paper. If you want to make your application look extra nice, you can print your cover letter and résumé on résumé paper. Résumé paper is sometimes also known as business or specialty paper, and it is thicker and rougher than regular printer paper. However, it's also more expensive, so you may not want to use it for every job application.

Mistakes To Avoid

There are several things job seekers can do in their cover letters that can *hurt* their chances of getting an interview. You will want to avoid these mistakes.

- ❖ Don't write "To Whom It May Concern" or "Dear Sir or Madam". If you don't know the person's name, use something generic and gender neutral, like *Candidate Selection Team* or *Dear Hiring Manager.*

- ❖ Don't use slang, like *I crushed the highest sales in my region three years running.*

❖ Don't use correction fluid or make corrections after a letter is printed. Reprint your letter if necessary.

❖ Don't write a letter that's longer than one page.

❖ Don't provide false information about yourself or your qualifications.

❖ Don't include erroneous information about a company.

❖ Don't include personal information (avoid references to religion, family, etc.).

❖ Don't write poorly (avoid using cliches, exaggeration, and typographical or grammatical errors).

❖ Don't use form letters and mass mailings. Each letter should be tailored to a specific job.

❖ Don't include photos unless it's specifically requested.

❖ Don't confess weakness or apologize for lacking a qualification.

❖ Don't use an improper tone (angry, demanding, desperate, confessional, or too enthusiastic).

❖ Don't include salary information unless it's requested.

I deserve to be happy in my career…

Affirm

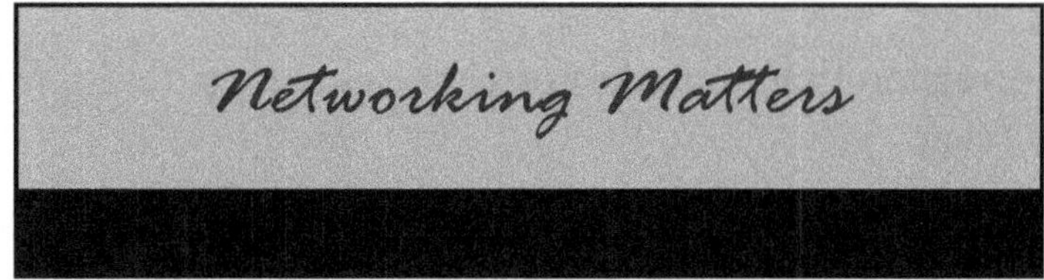

Networking is the process of making connections and is generally considered the best way to find a job. You can network with just about anyone, both in-person and online. Consider discussing your job search with friends and family, or with people you know from religious or recreational organizations. You can also talk to people you know professionally and academically or use social media sites like LinkedIn and Facebook to connect with others in your field.

Making polite and persistent direct contact with the people who influence hiring may increase your chances of being considered for a job. Try stopping by a company in person to present your résumé or talking with a receptionist or administrative assistant. If you've dropped off a résumé or work samples, you can send a brief follow-up email later on, or even introduce yourself to the hiring manager on a social media site.

If you can spare even a few hours a week, offer to volunteer for an employer in your field. You'll be able to gain critical work experience and make important contacts in your industry. Idealist.org offers a great introduction to volunteering for career development.

Many career fields have professional or trade associations that you can join to make connections and learn about job openings. The Internet can be a valuable tool for researching and finding opportunities. You can also use the Internet to find out which trade or professional associations are most popular in your field.

You may consider contacting a headhunter or recruiter to connect you with job openings at specific companies. Most headhunters and recruiters specialize in a specific industry like engineering or health care and are compensated by the company to find potential candidates. Always research the reputation of a headhunter or recruiter and be wary of anyone who asks for money to find you a job.

You may want to contact staffing and temporary agencies, which supply companies with temporary or contract workers. Temporary assignments may provide you with opportunities to make connections or gain permanent employment.

Job Search and Networking

Getting Started

Looking for a job takes a great deal of time, energy, and effort. Below are different things you will need to begin your job search.

- ❖ **Time**
  Preparing the necessary paperwork, researching opportunities, and networking can be time-consuming, especially if you currently have another job. Try developing a regular schedule for your job-hunting activities that makes the most efficient use of your time.

- ❖ **Internet Access**
  The Internet is essential to job hunting. If you do not have Internet access at home, you will need to arrange for regular access to the Internet at your public library, coffee shop, Internet cafe, or a friend's house.

- ❖ **Email Address**
  Establish a professional email address and avoid silly or inappropriate names. In addition, you should never use your current work email address to search for a new job. This practice is unprofessional and could even jeopardize your current employment. Sign up for a free webmail service like **Gmail** or **Outlook.com**.

- ❖ **Necessary Paperwork**
  Depending on your career goals, you may need to prepare job applications, online résumés, plain-text résumés, job-specific cover letters, portfolios, and thank you letters.

- ❖ **Additional items**
  Other items you may need include **business cards** for networking, a **professional-looking photo** for online networking, and materials for **organizing your search**, like a job search log.

Strategic Networking for the Job Search

Ask Questions

Asking a series of purposeful questions can help you engage someone you're meeting for the first time. Most people generally like talking about themselves, so don't shy away from asking about someone's career and interests. At this point, you should be focused on getting to know your new contact and how this person might fit into your network. You're not asking for a job, just more information.

Consider asking some of the following questions when you're meeting someone for the first time:

- ❖ How did you get started in your current career?
- ❖ What do you like most about your job? What are the biggest challenges you face?
- ❖ Would you choose the same career path if you had to do it all over again?

Craft Your Elevator Pitch

In busy social settings, you may only have a few moments to capture someone's attention or make an impression. One of the most effective ways to get your message across is to develop a personal elevator pitch. An elevator pitch is a clear and specific statement that describes you and your strengths in less than 30 seconds. Preparing your speech in advance can also help you feel more comfortable introducing yourself to new people. Your elevator pitch should explain who you are, what you're seeking, and what you can offer.

Sample Elevator Pitch

"I'm currently studying accessory design at fashion school, and I'm really interested in launching my own jewelry line after I graduate. Now, I'm seeking an internship to help me put what I'm learning into practice."

After you've composed your pitch, be sure to practice it by yourself and with friends until it sounds natural. Don't be afraid to modify your speech over time or adapt it for certain situations. Remember, your elevator pitch should leave someone wanting to know more about you. An introduction has the potential to become a more lengthy conversation or even a screening interview, so be prepared to talk about your experience and what you could contribute.

Build Relationships

How you conclude your first meeting with a new contact is vital to building an effective relationship. Even if your encounter is brief, make sure you leave it with a request to keep in touch, either by meeting again in person or connecting online through email or social media.

Remember, networking is a long-term investment that requires time and persistence. Most of the connections you make will not have anything to offer you initially. By politely following up with your contacts, you'll be able to develop a relationship over time. The stronger your relationships, the more likely it is that your connections will think of you when opportunities arise.

Who Is In Your Network?

- ❖ Family, friends, and their contacts
- ❖ Neighbors and their contacts
- ❖ Classmates and roommates
- ❖ Faculty and staff
- ❖ Current and former colleagues and supervisors
- ❖ Student organization members

Networking Resources

- ❖ **Business cards**. Believe it or not, paper business cards are still a great way to share your contact information quickly and easily. Your business card should be simple, with your **basic contact information** and a concise personal statement, such as a shorter version of your **elevator pitch** (no more than a few sentences). If you feel comfortable using new technologies, there are many **mobile apps** that can help you scan and share business cards.
- ❖ **Networking log**. You'll need to make sure you have an organized system for maintaining and tracking your connections so you can effectively **follow up** and **maintain contact**.

Americans deal with a recession in the US economy every 7-10 years.

Do It Yourself

Take some time to reflect on the following questions as you begin building your network:

1. Who is in your current network?

2. How can you expand your network? Can you join social or professional organizations for networking?

3. How will you introduce yourself to new people? What is your elevator pitch?

4. What can you offer new connections to build a mutually beneficial relationship?

5. What tools will you use to keep up with your connections?

Once you've started looking for a job, there are different **strategies** that can make your search more effective. In a constantly evolving society with an ever-competitive job market, no one job search strategy guarantees positive results. Conducting a job search is not easy. A good job search requires on-going preparation, commitment, and hard work. It can be challenging, exciting, and discouraging all at the same time.

Simply finding a job to put food on the table is shortsighted. For the long term, one needs a job to prepare for the next job, and the next and the next. This means you have to find a way to match your skills with an employer's needs. You must show how your education and previous work experience relate to an employment opportunity.

Review the techniques below to learn more about getting the most out of your job search.

>>> *Staying Motivated*

Searching for a job can be a difficult and lengthy process. Even after you've adopted the right mindset and started using a variety of job search strategies, it can be difficult to stay motivated if your search isn't going as well as you had hoped.

Try your best to stay positive and set goals for your job-hunting activities. Goals can help you measure your progress and add structure to your job search. You might also consider creating a support network of friends and family members who are also looking for new opportunities. You'll be able to share your experiences and help encourage one another to keep searching.

>>> *Following Up*

Another common quality among successful job seekers is a willingness to follow up. Just making a connection or submitting your résumé is simply not enough to help you stand out among other possible candidates. Following up will give you the opportunity to show your interest, assert your qualifications, and establish a positive relationship with the person who may ultimately hire you.

While it's important not to be overly aggressive in pursuing opportunities, following up in a timely, professional, and courteous manner will simply underscore your interest in the position, making a positive impression on your potential employer.

>>> *Staying Organized*

After you've started your job search, you'll understand how important it will be to develop a way to keep everything organized. Imagine how embarrassing it might be to receive a call from a hiring manager and not remember who he is or how you met. You might consider creating a job search log, where you can document your job search, make a list of potential connections, and keep track of the jobs you have applied for.

Conducting An Effective Online Job Search

The Internet has made it easier than ever to discover new opportunities. There are hundreds of websites that allow you to search for job postings and upload your résumé, such as Indeed and CareerBuilder. While these sites have dramatically changed the way we look for jobs, they cannot be used in isolation.

Online job searching is most useful when combined with other job search methods, such as networking and direct contact with employers. As a result, you will need to make the most of the time you spend searching online. Review the techniques below to learn how to conduct an effective online job search.

Using Job Search Engines And Job Alerts

Rather than search through various websites, you can use a job search engine such as Indeed or SimplyHired. Job search engines collect job listings from hundreds of websites so you can view them in a single place.

As with any search engine, the key is to optimize the number of relevant results you obtain, so you may have to experiment with search terms and refinements. Indeed's Job Search Tips gives great advice about how to get started.

You can also save time by creating a job alert. A job alert is a summary of new job postings from a specific search that is sent to your email. Receiving only a few job listings each day will allow you to stay current with the latest opportunities without having to sort through a long list of search results.

Additional Job Search Sites

While job search engines are one of the easiest ways to find a variety of job postings, you may also want to take advantage of more specific websites, depending on your needs.

- ❖ GlassDoor is one of the most internationally focused job-hunting sites available today. You can search for jobs at specific companies around the world and read employee reviews to learn what it's like to work for different employers.

- ❖ Social media sites like LinkedIn, Facebook, and Twitter have become increasingly valuable tools for finding jobs online.

- ❖ Salary.com Salary Wizard gives you the tools to understand your worth. Get your free personalized salary and start your salary comparison by location, industry, benefits, and pay factors in Salary Wizard.

Posting Your Résumé Online

Some sites allow you to post your résumé online. When employers need to fill a job opening, they can search through online résumés to find a candidate that fits their needs. This can increase your chances of finding a job because employers will have the ability to search for you. Some sites will also use the information in your résumé to automatically send you relevant job postings.

There are some potential downsides to posting your résumé online. For example, you risk exposing yourself to unwanted contact, spam, and privacy concerns. If you are job hunting and currently employed, you may want to avoid posting your résumé. If your employer finds your résumé, it could possibly lead to termination. Be sure to weigh the pros and cons before deciding to post your résumé online.

Responding To An Online Job Posting

Once you've found a job that you'd like to apply for, it's important to take the right approach when responding to the job posting. Your response will directly affect the employer's decision to contact you for an interview. Here are some things you can do to improve an online job application:

- ❖ Research the employer online and read through their company website, if available. This will help you to determine if the job posting is genuine. It will also be helpful to know as much as you can about the employer when you are applying and interviewing for the position.

- ❖ Make sure that your résumé is up-to-date and clearly demonstrates how your skills relate to the position you are applying for. You should also add more detail to your most relevant work experience and emphasize why your work history qualifies you for the position.

- ❖ Your cover letter should explain why you are a good fit for the position. You can edit a cover letter that you've already used for another application, but make sure you tailor it specifically to the position. Some employers use computer software to screen initial applicants, so be sure to include specific phrases found in the job posting. This will prevent you from being automatically excluded from certain positions.

❖ A résumé and cover letter need to look professional, which means that they must be free of any spelling or grammatical errors. Your computer's spell-checker won't catch everything, so be sure to double-check your résumé and cover letter before sending them off. You can also ask a friend to read through them to see if you've missed anything.

❖ Some online job postings will ask you to send your résumé and cover letter by email, while others will direct you to an online application. If you are submitting your résumé and cover letter by email, you should paste them into the body of the email and include them as attachments.

❖ If you don't hear from the employer within a week of sending your application, send them an email or call to make sure they have received your application and to restate your interest in the position.

Staying Safe Online

Always remember to exercise your best judgment online, especially when looking for a job. The Internet is a powerful resource for finding new opportunities, but not every job posting you'll find is genuine. Many of these fake postings are actually an attempt to steal money and sensitive information from job seekers. The following tips can help you guard your privacy and avoid potential scams during your job search.

Protecting Your Identity And Avoiding Scams

❖ Never share sensitive information online, such as your Social Security Number, birth date, or credit card number. If a potential employer asks you to send this kind of information, the odds are high that the employer is simply trying to steal your identity rather than offer you a job.

❖ Be wary of anyone who asks you to pay for something like training or a background check before offering you a position.

❖ Avoid jobs that seem suspicious or promise a high salary for a minimal amount of work. Any job that sounds too good to be true probably is.

Legitimate job postings will usually contain the name of the company, specific details about the job, and information about who to contact and how to apply for the position. Some of this may vary by field, though. For example, government jobs in the US do not always have a specific contact person listed.

❖ If you feel uneasy or suspicious about a job posting, follow your instincts and research it for more information. If the posting turns out to be a hoax, you'll keep yourself from wasting a lot of time and energy on the application.

*Studies show that Americans change
jobs every 4-5 years.*

Career Connection 2.0

Build My Personal Brand

There is no professional development without personal development first. Same with your professional and personal brand. Your professional brand reflects your personal brand. What do you stand for? What do you represent? What do others think about when they think of you? How do others feel when they think about you and what you have to offer? Every time you post on social media it's a reflection of who you are and what you represent.

Your current brand—or reputation—is built on a series of comments, actions, outfits, or accomplishments. It's not what you do one day to create a personal brand; it's what you do every day.

Personal Branding

The idea of personal branding has become increasingly popular among job seekers and professionals over the past several years. But what exactly is personal branding? Simply put, branding is how you present yourself to others. Everyone already has their own brand identity: the qualities that make them different and unique. The process of personal branding gives you an opportunity to discover, strengthen, and market those qualities.

I am worthy of the career success I desire...

Affirm

Building Your Personal Brand

There are several factors you will need to consider as you begin developing your own personal brand. Rather than inventing a false persona, your brand should be an authentic expression of who you are, what you value, and what you want to accomplish. Taking the time to determine your values, passions, and skills will help you create a personal brand that is both memorable and genuine.

Instead of starting from scratch, your brand should be informed by your existing reputation. Think about how your current friends and colleagues would describe you and your personality. You can strengthen and emphasize these qualities as you develop your personal brand.

Your brand will also be determined by the audience you are attempting to reach and influence. Different fields will value certain skills above others. For example, an elementary school teacher might create a very different personal brand than someone working as a sales manager or an engineer. It's all about discovering how best to connect with the people who matter to you and your brand.

Even if you're not freelancing or running a business, it's important to have a personal brand...

Clarity Questions

---

1. **Your Niche**. What are you really good at?

2. **Your Story**. How did you get to be good at it?

3. **Your Values**. How do you approach your work?

3. **Your Offering**. How can you solve your clients or employer problems?

Building Your Brand

As employers start to rely on social media and online resources for screening and recruiting potential candidates, it's especially important for your brand to have a strong online presence. But there's still more to your brand than how you market yourself online. As you work to develop your online brand, you should also be thinking about how you can promote your brand when meeting people directly. Below are some ways to monitor and build your personal brand.

- ❖ **Google Yourself.** Before you start promoting your brand online, you should take some time to learn about your current online reputation. Search for your own name on a search engine like Google and see what kind of information comes up.

- ❖ **Email Address**. Make sure that your email address reflects a professional image. Try using a simple version of your name and profession (coach.alicesmith@gmail.com for example), rather than something too casual.

- ❖ Social media sites like **Facebook, Twitter, Meetup, and YouTube** are a great way to share your brand with as many people as you can. Upload the same profile photo to different social media sites so you'll be easily identifiable across your networks.

- ❖ **LinkedIn**. With over 175 million members worldwide, LinkedIn is the largest social media site for professional networking. Customizing your profile picture, headline, and choosing a custom URL can help you be more noticeable on LinkedIn.

- ❖ **Elevator Pitch**. An elevator pitch is a clear and specific statement that summarizes you and your brand in under thirty seconds.

- ❖ **Business Card**. Paper business cards are still a great way to share your contact information quickly and easily. Your business card should be simple with your basic contact information and a concise personal statement like a shorter version of your elevator pitch (no more than a few sentences).

❖ **Résumé**. Even if you don't have an opportunity to meet a potential employer directly, your résumé is another great place to communicate your brand identity. A strong résumé can help you stand out from other candidates.

Maintaining Your Personal Brand

Once you've established your brand, you'll need to keep working to project a strong and consistent brand identity. Remember that actions speak louder than words—be sure to follow through on the promises associated with your brand. For example, if you brand yourself as a hard-working and reliable person, coming in late or neglecting your work doesn't help to reinforce your brand image.

Your brand will need to be flexible as you move between various positions and career paths, so don't be afraid to make changes to your brand as needed. Even if you've accomplished an initial goal, such as finding a new job, it's important to assess your brand from time to time. Some parts of your brand that were once relevant may need to be updated; refreshing your brand identity can help you build new relationships and advance your career.

I am creating my career success...

Affirm

Linkedin is a popular social network with a specific purpose. While other social networks like Facebook and Twitter focus more on your personal life, LinkedIn is all about professional networking—that is, building a group of contacts to help advance your career. More and more businesses use LinkedIn to screen and recruit potential employees. This is why creating a LinkedIn account can make a difference when searching for your next job. Once you've signed up, you can add information to your profile page, which is a brief summary of your skills and employment history that effectively serves as an online résumé.

To build your network, you can add contacts (also known as connections) with other LinkedIn users. As you make connections, you'll be able to get skill endorsements, ask for recommendations, and find new job opportunities.

You can also join groups focused on various companies, industries, and occupations. Groups can keep you up to date on the latest news in your field, as well as help you find others who share your professional interests.

LinkedIn has a powerful job search tool that can find openings around the world. You can then filter these results by company, experience level, and more. Some openings also have an Easy Apply option, which allows you to apply to a job with only a few clicks by submitting the information in your LinkedIn profile.

From making first impressions with employers to communicating with colleagues, LinkedIn can be a useful career tool. Fortunately, creating an account is free, and it only requires your email address.

If you take the time to learn how to use LinkedIn, it can make a big impact on your professional life.

Creating A LinkedIn Account

Creating a LinkedIn account is simple. All you need is an email address and a few minutes of your time. Let's take a look at how it works.

To get started, go to linkedin.com in your web browser. Enter your information, choose a password, and then click the Join button. LinkedIn will guide you through the steps of adding more detail to your profile.

Next, you'll need to verify your email address. Go to your email inbox, look for a message from LinkedIn, then click the confirmation button or type the PIN into LinkedIn. It may also ask for your phone number to send you another verification code, so you may want to have your phone nearby just in case.

Syncing Email Contacts And Other Information

You can also choose to sync the contacts list from your email account. This will make it easier for you to find people you already know on LinkedIn. You can always click skip if you'd rather do this later.

LinkedIn will also ask for information about yourself, such as your most recent job title, location, and profile photo. Like with email contacts, you can skip some of these steps if you'd rather deal with them later. However, I recommend exploring everything LinkedIn has to offer to ensure you're getting the most out of it.

Choosing a Basic or Premium Account

Finally, you may be asked to choose between a Basic account (which is free) and a Premium account (which has a monthly subscription fee). Because you're getting started with LinkedIn, I recommend using the Basic account for now. While a Premium account provides additional features like additional messaging options and job opening details, I've found that you can get quite a lot from LinkedIn using just the Basic account. You can always upgrade to a Premium account later if you want.

That's it! Your account is now set up, and you're ready to create your profile and start adding connections.

Creating Your Profile

Your profile is one of the most important things on LinkedIn, especially because it's the first thing people will see when they find you on the site. You should treat your profile as you would a résumé, taking the time to make sure it is complete, accurate, and professional. LinkedIn also allows you to add things you might not include on a traditional résumé, like a profile picture and personal summary.

Adding Profile Information

The process of changing your LinkedIn profile is fairly straightforward. Once you understand how to add job entries and edit your education history, it should be much easier to focus on the information itself.

Adding A Profile Picture

A high-quality profile picture can make a big difference to potential employers. That's why we strongly recommend adding one to your profile before searching for jobs on LinkedIn.

Tips For An Effective Profile

Keep in mind that there's no right or wrong way to use LinkedIn, so you'll need to experiment to find what works for you.

- ❖ **Keep your profile up to date**. Make sure the information on your LinkedIn profile is updated and consistent with the details on your résumé. This will make it easier for an employer to match your résumé with your LinkedIn profile. Also, because a

LinkedIn profile doesn't have length restrictions, you can even add details and positions you can't fit on your résumé.

- ❖ **Add relevant skills**. LinkedIn makes it easy to add skills to your profile page. Examples of skills you might add include problem solving, strong communication, and computer software—think Microsoft Office, Photoshop, QuickBooks, and so on. Your connections can even endorse you for the skills you've added to your profile.

- ❖ **Ask for recommendations**. A recommendation is a short comment written by another LinkedIn member that will appear on your profile. When seeking a recommendation, try to reach out to people who are familiar with your talents, skills, and performance in the workplace

Adding Connections

Adding connections is a big part of LinkedIn. But unlike most other social media sites, trying to connect with everyone you know can send the wrong signal. Doing so can seem like you're networking for its own sake rather than truly building your professional network. Before you add someone to your network, ask yourself: Would this person talk to me about a job or recommend me to an employer?

If the answer is yes, then it may be a good idea to add this person as a connection.

To add connections on LinkedIn, select My Network at the top of the screen. A list of people you may know will appear, along with any connection invitations you may have. If you see someone you'd like to connect with, simply click Connect. You can also search for someone and click Connect on their profile.

Tips When Adding Connections

- ❖ **Use your existing network**. When you first create a LinkedIn profile, make sure to connect with the people you already know. Try syncing your email contacts and using LinkedIn's search bar to find friends, classmates, and coworkers.

- ❖ **Ask for introductions**. If you're trying to connect with someone you've never met, you should look to see if you have any mutual connections. If so, you can ask your connections for an introduction. Be polite and explain why you are requesting the introduction and give your connection an opportunity to decline the request.

- ❖ **Maintain your connection**. After connecting with someone, remember to keep engaging with that person on LinkedIn. If they post status updates, leave thoughtful comments. If they ask for recommendations or endorsements, try to fulfill their request in a timely manner. This should strengthen your connection, which could lead to new opportunities.

Searching For Jobs On LinkedIn

When it comes to searching for jobs, LinkedIn can be a powerful resource. It allows employers to post job openings to the site (like any online job board), and you can search for these openings using the job search tool. LinkedIn also allows you to use your connections to find new positions and ask for recommendations. Additionally, you can follow companies so you'll always be notified of their latest LinkedIn posts.

Using The Job Search Tool

Because employers frequently use LinkedIn to screen and recruit potential candidates, more and more companies have begun posting job openings to the site. This is why it's so important to learn how to use LinkedIn's job search tool.

To search for jobs, click the Jobs icon, then type what you're looking for in the search box. You can also narrow your search results by using the filters near the top of the window, like company, recent postings, and experience level.

If you want to apply to the job, click Apply, and you'll be taken to the company's website to fill out an application. Some openings also have an Easy Apply option, which allows you to apply to a job with just a few clicks by submitting the information in your LinkedIn profile. Keep in mind that if you use Easy Apply, I recommend writing a personalized cover letter with every application you send.

You can also set up preferences for your job search through the career interests function. From your profile, scroll down until you find Your Dashboard, then click career interests.

This lets you save preferences for the type of job you're looking for, including location, company size, and industry. LinkedIn will then start giving you relevant recommendations and search results. I suggest using career interests so you'll have a better chance of seeing jobs you're actually interested in.

Real-World Application 

Navigate to the LinkedIn.com website or download LinkedIn app and create a profile using the steps given to create an account.

"Success isn't about how much money you make; it's about the difference you make in people's lives."
Michelle Obama

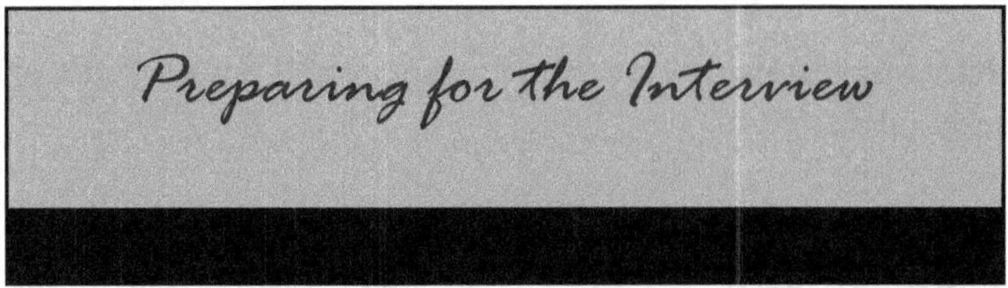

The job interview is one of the most important stages in the recruitment process; when the employer asks you "Why should I hire you?", he or she wants to know what exactly recommends you as the perfect candidate. However, when you meet your potential employer face to face, you may experience a certain degree of uneasiness that may alter your communication skills, especially if you do not have the experience in interviewing for a job. If you want to avoid panic, you have to prepare yourself in advance.

Companies like candidates who know what they want from a job. They are also impressed with someone who has done research before arriving at the interview. Make the effort to look into the organization you're interested in, and you'll find yourself ahead of the competition.

To get a sense of how the organization you're interested in sees itself, go to their website and read about the company's history and plans for the future. Company websites, along with their official social media pages, often have employee photos or posts about the business, both of which will give you some idea of the company culture. You can also read the company's brochures and annual reports if they've been made publicly available. No matter the size of the company, you can do a web search for the organization's name and read any articles that may have mentioned the company. For example, you may discover that the organization was recently involved in a charitable event—or a lawsuit.

You may also be interested to find out what other people think about the organization you're interested in. These days, most organizations are rated and reviewed by online users in some way. Just be wary about what you're reading because anyone can post an opinion, whether it's an accurate representation or not. As you do this research, you can begin to develop questions and take them with you to the interview.

Common Interview Questions

1. Tell me about yourself.

2. Why are you interested in working for this company?

3. Tell me about your education.

4. Why have you chosen this particular field?

5. In a job, what interests you most/least?

6. What is your major weakness?

7. Give an example of how you solved a problem in the past.

8. What do you consider your best accomplishment in your last job?

9. If you were hired, what ideas/talents could you contribute to the position or our company?

10. Do you have any questions for me?

Questions To Ask The Employer

1. What are the responsibilities of this position?

2. What is the history of the position?

3. Why is it vacant?

4. What are the key challenges or problems of this position?

5. When and how will I be evaluated?

6. What are the performance standards?

7. With whom would I be working?

8. Who would be my supervisor?

9. What is the department's environment like?

10. When will you make the hiring decision?

Illegal Questions

1. Have you ever filed a Workers' Compensation claim or been injured on the job?

2. Do you have any physical conditions that would prevent you from performing the job?

3. Have you ever been hospitalized?

4. Have you ever been treated by a psychiatrist or psychologist?

5. How many days were you absent from work because of illness last year?

6. Are you taking any prescribed drugs?

7. Have you ever been treated for drug addiction or alcoholism?

Making the Rounds

First-Round Interviews

Most initial or "first round" interviews last 30-45 minutes and are often 1-on-1 or 2-on-1. The emphasis is to get to know your motivations and goals better, while gathering specific information about the experiences and skills already highlighted in your application.

First 2–3 minutes: Introductions, small talk, what to expect

Next 15–20 minutes: Questions for you

Final 5–10 minutes: Questions for the interviewer, next steps

Second-Round Interviews

Some organizations make hiring decisions based on one interview, but several rounds of interviews are the norm, including a visit to the organization itself. Interviews that take place at the organization can last a few hours to a full day, and you are likely to meet with a number of people from the department in which you would work, and potentially employees from different departments.

Questions to Ask

To best prepare for these interviews, ask the recruiter or hiring manager these questions:

1. What is the overall agenda for my interview?

2. With whom will I be interviewing?

3. Are there any materials or information you would like me to bring?

Salaries & Offers

You've polished your résumé and tailored your cover letter. You've practiced your interviewing skills. You've even picked out the right attire to wear. Don't step into the interview, however, without thinking about potential salaries and what is standard pay for the position or industry.

Timing is Everything

Choose the right time to talk about salary. Unless asked specifically, do not mention compensation until you have secured an offer. Throughout the application and interview process, you want to focus on showing the employer your qualifications and determining whether or not the position is a good fit. Decide ahead of time what is acceptable. Consider the minimum compensation that you would accept and what you would like to receive. Do your research. Find out the average salary range for the type of work you're seeking.

Evaluate the entire package, not just the salary amount. Your base salary is very important, but a comprehensive benefits package can add 30–40%. This can include health care premiums, retirement contributions, personal time off, tuition reimbursement and professional association fees. Consider your future earnings potential, which can increase significantly with future bonuses, commissions, or promotions. Intangible benefits are important to consider as well.

I am confident and calm in interviews…

Affirm

Job Interview Tips

Know Yourself

During an interview, your job is to sell yourself, so you need to know your skills well enough to do this effectively. Connecting your skills with the company's needs is the best way to get hired. List your accomplishments and then think of which skills it took to do them. Review your skills list and refine it into a "package" you can explain easily in a minute or two. And don't forget to sell yourself as a person. Most organizations want honest, smart, friendly, motivated, and responsible employees. Do you deal well with people? Are you smart? Self-motivated?

Practice, Practice, Practice

You can make all the lists you want, but there's no substitute for rehearsing how you'll handle an interview. Ask your parent, sibling, or friend to be the interviewer, and give him or her a list of questions to throw at you, especially the hard ones. You will benefit and gain confidence from having thought about the answers, and you may be able to apply them to questions that you didn't anticipate.

If you get a question you can't answer, simply say you don't know. Then say the question is something to which you would like to give more thought and that you are willing to learn what it takes. An employer will respect someone who is honest and open about his or her limitations.

In addition, be aware of your body language. If you can record yourself on video, use it for practice. Otherwise a mirror will do, or get feedback from your parent, sibling, or friend.

Hand and arm movements shouldn't be too large. Don't fiddle, shake your leg, or tap your fingers. This is unprofessional and may distract your potential employer. Your posture should be relaxed, but alert. Don't slouch; if you look bored the interviewer will assume you'd be bored in the job, too. Communicate interest and energy. Be yourself. Your potential employer knows you're nervous but try not to make it so obvious that it becomes a distraction.

Dress The Part

Looking professional means looking respectable. Check the company's website for pictures of the employees to give you an idea of the overall dress code. While a suit is nearly always appropriate in a corporate setting, sometimes it does not make sense for the organization. Whatever you choose to wear, it should be clean, ironed, coordinated and appropriate.

Skirts should not be above the knee; shirts should not be cut too low and jewelry should be moderate. Shirts should also cover the entire shoulder—no tank tops. Even employers who don't ask that their employees dress up will appreciate that you've chosen to put your best foot forward.

As for footwear, sneakers and flip-flops should stay at home. Wearing open-toed shoes may be fashionable, but they're not appropriate before you get the job. Depending on what you've learned about the company dress code, it might be a good idea to remove piercings (aside from small, traditional earrings) and make sure any tattoos are concealed under your clothing.

Personal grooming is part of your "dress" too. Be sure to freshen up before your interview, but don't overwhelm your potential employer with your favorite perfume or cologne. Take extra time to feel confident about your appearance and it will be one less thing that stands between you and your dream job.

On some occasions, an employer will call you back for a second interview. Think positively and plan ahead—make sure you have a few professional outfits.

Arrive Early

It may seem obvious, but if you're not on time for your interview, the game is over. Getting there early makes a good impression on the interviewer and allows you to take a few deep breaths, organize your notes, refresh your memory on any points that you've found difficult in your practices and scan any company materials that may be available in the waiting room. It also allows you to use the restroom if needed, freshen your breath, and make any last-minute appearance adjustments.

Whatever your mode of transportation, make sure you have directions to your target organization, along with a backup route, in case of unexpected obstacles like traffic or a subway delay. Also, have the telephone number of someone to notify in case you're running late.

If you can, perform a dry run a few days before your interview: Travel to your target organization and be sure you know how to get there—to the door—without getting lost. Planning ahead means you'll feel better about yourself, and you'll be more relaxed in the interview.

Be Yourself

In the interview, let your true personality shine through. Trained interviewers spot actors quickly, and they are unlikely to hire anyone they feel they can't trust. Be proud of the unique collection of talents, motivations and skills that make you the individual you are. Believe in your ability to learn, grow, develop. Show "the real you" and you'll be well on your way to getting hired.

I am dependable and do my job well...

Affirm

Ask Questions

Usually at the end of an interview, you'll be asked if you have any questions. If you don't ask something, it can be taken as a sign of lack of preparation or interest. So prepare some questions before the interview and take notes during the interview to keep track of questions you might want to ask.

There are two areas you should inquire about—the organization and the job itself. Are you clear on the responsibilities of the job? If not, ask for clarification. Do you see where the job fits into the structure of the organization? What is the working environment like? Is there a path for advancement?

If all else fails and you can't think of what to ask, check your notes and ask your interviewer for clarification or further detail about something he or she has already brought up. It will show that you were paying attention and were interested in what he or she had to tell you. If it seems appropriate, ask your interviewer what his or her favorite thing or least favorite thing about working at this company is—you may learn about something you wouldn't have otherwise known.

Be sure you know what the next steps are after the interview. Are they going to contact you? When do they think they will do that? Would they prefer that you follow up with them? How is the best way to do that?

The end of the interview is also a good time to emphasize how interested you are in taking the process to the next step and why you think you're the perfect candidate for the job. You can reinforce this sentiment by asking your interviewer for his or her business card so that you can be in touch with him or her. But don't beg for the job; let your positive attitude and enthusiasm speak for you. Upon leaving, make sure to shake the person's hand again and make sincere eye contact. And, of course, don't forget to thank him or her.

Follow Up

Your interview isn't over when you walk out the door. As soon as you get home, write a short thank-you note to your interviewer. Tell him or her that you appreciated the time he or she spent with you and the chance to learn more about the job and the organization. Traditionally, a thank-you note refers to a neatly handwritten card mailed to the organization's address, but it is equally acceptable (and expected) to send a thank-you email to your interviewer. If you promised to send something additional—writing samples or another copy of your résumé, for example—make sure to enclose it. Keep your note short and restate your understanding of the next step.

Be sure to follow through. If you say in your note that you'll give them a follow-up, call on Tuesday, be sure to do so. If you'd like to add something you forgot to say in the interview, this is the time and place. If you did not obtain your interviewer's business card before you left, find another way to be sure that you spell his or her name(s) correctly. If it can't be found on the company website or LinkedIn, call the receptionist to have him or her spell it for you. Unless told otherwise, keep in contact with the human resources representative after your interview and consider sending him or her a thank-you note as well.

You'd be surprised how many candidates never offer this simple courtesy. Send a thank-you note and you'll stand out in the crowd.

The Bureau of Labor Statistics (BLS) reported that 3.2 million Americans voluntarily quit their job in December 2017 and that more than 20 percent of workers leave their new employer within the first 45 days.

Clarity Questions

---

1. What do you want your paychecks to allow you to do?

2. What does your target lifestyle cost?

3. When do you have "enough"? What factors could affect that?

4. What would you do if someone gave you an extra $ 15,000 tomorrow?

Hired: Meet Employer Expectations

I Got the Job, Now What

Once you get the job, you might think the hard part is over, and you can relax. That couldn't be more wrong. Finding the right job is hard work. Keeping it can be even harder-but only when you're not prepared. The good news is that you can avoid many problems through how you prepare yourself and what you do in your daily job performance. This is especially true when you begin a new job. You're starting fresh. You're excited and full of hope. The person who hired you feels the same way. You both want to prove that the decision to hire you was wise.

Three Major Employer Expectations

First you must understand what your employer wants from you. In general, most managers expect employees to be:

Be Dependable. Employers expect employees to show up for work on time and be honest & reliable.

Be Professionally Dressed And Groomed. Employers expect employees to be clean, neat, and professional in their appearance and follow dress codes.

Be Skilled. Employers expect employees to have the necessary skills, experience, and credentials to properly do the job.

Why People Get Fired

Another way to think about how to succeed comes from thinking about why people don't succeed. People lose their jobs because they:

- Are unreliable and absent or late too many days
- Cannot get along with other workers or their supervisors
- Refuse to follow orders
- Lie on their résumé or applications
- Steal from the employers
- Have unacceptable grooming or clothes
- Use work time for personal business
- Cannot do the work, work too slowly, or make too many mistakes
- Do not follow safety rules

I have plenty to offer and contribute to my job…

Affirm

Clarity Questions

---

1. Do you meet your employer's expectations? If not, what can you do to become the type of employee your supervisor wants?

2. Do you have trouble with any of the issues listed?

3. Would your former supervisors use any of those reasons to describe your employment history?

Report to Work on Time

A 2011 survey by careerbuilder.com showed that 27 percent of the workers surveyed were late at least once a month. The most common reasons they gave included being held up in traffic (31 percent), oversleeping (18 percent), dealing with bad weather (11 percent), and taking children to school or daycare (8 percent). Other reasons included delays in public transportation, pets, spouses, and television and internet usage. About a third of the employers surveyed said they have had to fire employees for being late.

When you accept a new job, you are making a promise to be there. And when you're there, you're making a promise to do your work.

Solve Your Scheduling Problems

The first step in solving scheduling problems is to prevent them in the first place. Follow these guidelines:

- ❖ Make sure that you understand when you are supposed to be at work. Double-check any posted work schedules and return from meals or other breaks on time. Pay attention during holidays or particularly busy times because your regular schedule may change.
- ❖ If you have a problem with your work schedule, discuss it with your supervisor right away. Go to the discussion prepared with solutions for how the scheduling conflict will be resolved, such as switching shifts with a coworker.
- ❖ Follow the procedures for requesting time off. Know that there may be times when your employer cannot give you the time off that you want, and you will still have to come to work.

Make a Plan for Your Life Outside of Work

Keeping all personal business away from work can be difficult. From time to time, you may need to have your car repaired, arrange for someone to fix an appliance at your home, or handle a variety of childcare responsibilities. Life happens, and work is not your only responsibility. Your challenge is to handle as many of these other duties as possible outside your job. Doing so will require planning.

If you have children, you may need to have a backup plan in place for their care. When your regular childcare falls through and you have a backup plan, you can quickly make the change-without missing work. The backup plan will ease your mind and prevent problems on the job.

If you have a family, you will want to look at your family schedule at the beginning of each week. Think ahead. Can you schedule appointments on your off days? If not, can you move those appointments to a lunch hour? Can a spouse, friend, or older child take care of something for you? If you can keep your work life and personal life separated, you will increase your chance for success on the job.

Be Honest

Dishonesty is one the reasons employees are fired. Lying on an application or résumé is grounds for dismissal. Taking an employer's property can also result in someone being fired. Those are obvious wrongs and may be unthinkable to you.

There are also small ways of being dishonest that can creep up on us all. Is it lying to report that you have completed more work than you really have? Is it stealing to take a handful of the paperclips or packages of sweetener from the office supply when you're running low on them at home? It's the little things that no one may catch you doing that can lead to your being comfortable with wrongs you once would never have considered doing.

Every single day, you have to make decisions about the kind of employee you will be. You have to choose between right and wrong. The choices you make determine the reputation you will have.

For example, most people have some days when they don't want to go to work. If you are having one of those days, you may be tempted to call in sick. But think about the effect your absence will have. When you are not at work, who has to do your work? Will your coworkers have to do more than their share to cover for you? Will someone else be called in from a planned day off to cover for you? Will customers have to wait longer for service? Will the work just pile up and be worse when you return?

Nobody wins when you miss work unexpectantly-including you. Use your sick days for when you really are ill. Otherwise, you risk damaging your reputation with your coworkers and supervisors.

Pay Attention to How You Look

Whether you agree or not, your dress and grooming communicate a message to others. For example, your appearance tells everyone around you whether you want to fit in or stand out. Little things really matter when it comes to fitting in with a work group.

Some workplaces have written dress codes, but many do not. To make a good impression, look for people who are doing well at your workplace and try to dress and groom in a similar way. If you are not sure, dress a little better than your coworkers, particularly in a new job. Wear clean and well pressed clothing and pay attention to your grooming and other details, like your shoes.

Your personal grooming affects your attitude and the way others act towards you. When you look the best, you can, you feel better about yourself. When you feel better about yourself, your attitude and relationships with others improve. Make sure you take a daily shower or bath, groom your hair, wear clean clothes and shoes. Wear little cologne, use deodorant, and limit your jewelry.

Monitor Your Progress

Ideally, all employers would be clear about what they expect from employees and would provide the necessary training, guidance, and feedback to help employees meet those expectations. But ultimately it is your responsibility to make sure that you are doing your job well.

Returning to My Own Goals

At the beginning of this Career Success Guide, you set your own goals. Look back at those goals now. Which of them have you made come true, or have begun to make come true?

____

____

What has helped you to get closer to your goals?

____

____

What can you do in the future to achieve your goals?

____

____

Have some of your goals changed? If yes, how?

____

____

A Letter to Myself from the Future...

Imagine yourself six months into the future. What will have happened by then? What changes will have taken place in your life during those six months? Or, if you prefer, you could project yourself even further (years) into the future. Write a letter to your present-day self from the future self that you have imagined.

Notes

Congratulations

You Have Completed the Career Success Guide

Celebrate Your Greatness

Additional Resources

Recommended Books

- ❖ **Wild Hair**: *A Courageous Woman's Guide to a Bold and Authentic Career* by Tracy J. Edmonds

- ❖ **Comeback Careers**: *Rethink, Refresh, Reinvent Your Success--At 40, 50, and Beyond* by Mika Brzezinski With Ginny Brzezinski

- ❖ **The Introvert's Complete Career Guide**: *From Landing a Job, to Surviving, Thriving, and Moving on Up* by Jane Finkle

- ❖ **The Art of Work** - *How to Make Work, Work for You!* by Janice Bryant Howroyd

- ❖ **Redefine Wealth for Yourself**: *How to Stop Chasing Money and Finally Live Your Life's Purpose* by Patrice Washington

- ❖ **Living Check to Monday**: *The Real Deal About Money, Credit and Financial Security* by Lynn Richardson

- ❖ **Job Interview Tips for Overcoming Red Flags**: *Winning Strategies, Examples, and Short Stories for People With Not-So-Hot Backgrounds* by Ronald L. Krannich

- ❖ **Never Too Late**: *The Adult Student's Guide to College* by Rebecca Klein-Collins

9 798463 916570